Alexander McKenzie

Memorial to the Men of Cambridge Who Fell in the First

Battle of the Revolutionary War

Alexander McKenzie

Memorial to the Men of Cambridge Who Fell in the First Battle of the Revolutionary War

ISBN/EAN: 9783337236953

Printed in Europe, USA, Canada, Australia, Japan

Cover: Foto ©ninafisch / pixelio.de

More available books at **www.hansebooks.com**

MEMORIAL

TO THE

MEN OF CAMBRIDGE

WHO FELL IN THE

FIRST BATTLE OF THE REVOLUTIONARY WAR.

———•———

SERVICES OF DEDICATION, Nov. 3, 1870.

`CAMBRIDGE:

PRESS OF JOHN WILSON AND SON.

1870.

JUSTIN A. JACOBS, Esq., City Clerk:

MY DEAR SIR, — I acknowledge with pleasure the receipt of the vote of the City Government concerning the address delivered at their request on the third inst., and beg leave to return my thanks for the kind terms in which the address is mentioned.

In accordance with their request, I have now the honor to furnish a copy of the address, and to submit it to their disposal.

I am, yours most truly,

ALEXANDER McKENZIE.

IN BOARD OF ALDERMEN, Nov. 30, 1870.

Referred to Alderman MARCH. Sent down for concurrence.

Attest: JUSTIN A. JACOBS, *City Clerk.*

IN COMMON COUNCIL, Dec. 7, 1870.

Concurred.

Attest : J. W. COTTON, *Clerk.*

NOTE.

THIS Publication embraces a detailed account of the proceedings of the City Government, and those who gave their assistance, in providing for the erection and dedication of a Monument in honor of those sons of Cambridge who fell in defence of the popular cause, on the memorable 19th of April, 1775, within the territorial limits of the town.

The Monument is placed in the ancient burial-ground, in front of the College, upon the spot where the remains of three of the patriots were buried. It is of Scotch granite, about ten feet in height, and presents a very beautiful and substantial appearance. It bears this inscription, prepared by the Rev. ALEXANDER McKENZIE:

> Erected by the City
> A. D., 1870.
> To the memory of
> JOHN HICKS,
> WILLIAM MARCY,
> MOSES RICHARDSON,
> Buried here.
> JASON RUSSELL,
> JABEZ WYMAN,
> JASON WINSHIP,
> Buried in Menotomy.
> MEN OF CAMBRIDGE
> Who fell in defence of the Liberty of the People,
> April 19, 1775.
>
> "O, what a glorious morning is this!"

The exercises at the dedication were held in the vestry of the First Parish Church, overlooking the burial-ground, on the 3d of November, 1870, and were attended by a large number of ladies and citizens, notwithstanding the unfavorable weather, which prevented the audience from assembling upon the ground where the Monument is placed.

The services of dedication consisted of Music by a choir, under the direction of GEORGE FISHER, Esq.; and Addresses by Hon. H. R. HARDING, Mayor of the city, and the Rev. ALEXANDER McKENZIE; — Rev. PLINY WOOD officiating as Chaplain.

The first official step towards the erection of a Memorial to those citizens who fell within the limits of the town on the day of the battle of Lexington, was taken by Alderman HORATIO G. PARKER, on the 14th of September last, who on that day introduced the necessary order to the Board of which he was a member. The order was adopted, without dissent, by both branches of the Government.

These proceedings, it is believed, will be regarded as a valuable contribution to the history of Cambridge.

J. S. M.

ALDERMAN PARKER'S ADDRESS.

ON the 14th September, 1870, Alderman Horatio G. Parker, of Ward One, submitted the following order to the Board of Aldermen : —

Ordered, That the Committee on the Soldiers' Monument be directed to place a suitable memorial of stone on the Old Burial Ground, in Ward One, — over the common grave of citizens of this town, who fell on the 19th of April, 1775, — at a cost not exceeding five hundred dollars, and that the expense thereof be charged to Incidental Expenses.

Mr. Parker said he had been requested by citizens of Cambridge to introduce the order.

The matter has been freshly brought to the minds of our people by the Reverend Alexander McKenzie, who, in his recent address at the dedication of our Soldiers' Monument, said, —

" Down this road were brought some of our own people who had fallen, and in the hurry and confusion of the time were thrown into a common trench in this graveyard, until a happier day should come and they might have a better burial. Tradition ascribes to General Warren, who had himself been

within a hair's breadth of death, the promise that these
fallen patriots should have the care which was due
them. That day has been long in coming. The
grave into which they were cast remains here unmarked. I trust it will not be thought alien to the
purpose of this occasion, if I turn aside to ask that
the administration of your Honor, into which falls the
renown of this day, will take to itself the further
privilege of erecting an appropriate stone over the
place where the earlier patriotic dead of Cambridge
have been waiting so long."

Those earlier patriotic dead of Cambridge, Mr.
Mayor, fell April 19, 1775, the day of the battle of
Lexington. They, in their earnestness to hunt and
harass the King's troops, got between the British main
body and flank guard; and there were shot dead.

At night, after the British troops had fled, the
bodies of these men were brought down the West
Cambridge road, and across our Common to the graveyard, where their terrified and agonized relatives and
neighbors hastily dug for them a common grave. Into
that common grave they were thrown, their only
covering their bloody battle garments. And so they
were buried.

It was the first burial of men who fell in arms in
our eight years' Revolutionary War; and the men and
women who stood by, holding the torches and viewing
the sad sight, felt keenly and bitterly the want of
those common methods and furnishings by which we
endeavor to show our respect and affection for the
worthy dead.

General Warren endeavored to comfort those neighbors, friends, and relatives, by saying to them that the troubles of the land would soon be over, peace would come, and the proper thing should be done in memory and honor of those whom now they must so bury. In less than two months, General Warren had himself gloriously fallen, in the same manner, in the same cause; and his promise descended with his honors to the generations following.

Nearly one hundred years ago, Mr. Mayor, those men fell and were thus buried, and General Warren so promised; and that promise remains unfulfilled, that common grave remains unmarked to this day.

The people of Cambridge desire that this should be so no longer. They are eager that this duty of in some appropriate way designating and marking that common grave of our citizens, who fell on the day of the battle of Lexington, should be at once performed.

Our people recognize in this a patriotic duty too long neglected; and they feel it a pleasure that, while they shall discharge this their duty, they shall at the same time fulfil the proper and sympathizing promise of General Warren.

DEDICATION.

THE exercises were opened by the Rev. PLINY WOOD, who addressed the Throne of Grace in a fervent manner; calling upon the Giver of Good to bless the occasion, that it might awaken in every heart the desire to perpetuate the memory which clusters around the names of the patriot dead, who resisted to their death the efforts of Great Britain to place a yoke upon the necks of the people.

Following the Chaplain, a select choir of ten voices, under the direction of GEORGE FISHER, Esq., rendered the beautiful prayer from " Moses in Egypt." This concluded, Mayor HARDING addressed the audience.

REMARKS OF THE HON. H. R. HARDING.

When, some four months ago, we dedicated the Monument which stands on yonder Common, we were reminded by the Orator of that day of a duty which had long been neglected, but which it was not yet too late to perform. He recalled to our memories the events of that early period of our history, when resistance to British oppression began on these shores, and when our ancestors first met the enemies of liberty in the deadly contest which ended with the establishment here of a great Republic. He painted in vivid colors the circumstances which preceded and attended the first battle of the Revolution : how the midnight messengers hurried along these roads, bearing the fearful tidings that the troops of King George were on the march to pillage, to burn, and to murder ; how the drums beat to arms, and the warning bells summoned patriotic men to the stern duties of the battle-field ; how " women clustered together in their agony, alarmed for the fate of their husbands and sons, hearing the distant firing, then looking upon the battle as it came nearer, sure that some hearts were to break, some homes to be made desolate." He told us, further, how some of our own people who had fallen were brought down this road — now North Avenue — and were buried here in this graveyard in a common trench, where they should await happier days for a more suitable interment. From that day — so sad, and yet so glorious — until the present, there has been no attempt to fulfil the pledge given by General Warren, that these fallen patriots should have the care that was due them. From that day to this no stone has marked their burial-place, no inscription has informed the passing traveller that here lie buried the remains of those who died for country and for the rights of man.

Thanks to the reverend and patriotic gentleman who spoke to us on the occasion that I have referred to, and who will speak to us to-day ; thanks also to the City Council, which responded with alacrity to

the suggestions of our friend, — we are no longer to
rest under the stigma of having forgotten the services
of the men who perished in that earliest contest, or
of neglecting to mark the spot where their mortal
remains were deposited. Early in the month of September last, Alderman Parker, of the First Ward,
offered an order, in the branch of which he is a member, instructing the Committee on the Soldiers' Monument to procure and set up in this burial-ground a
memorial stone to commemorate the deeds and the
names of the Cambridge citizens who fell on the 19th
of April, 1775. The order was unanimously adopted
in both branches of the Government, and the Committee proceeded to attend to the duty which had
been imposed upon them. They selected a plain and
simple shaft of Scotch granite, and caused a suitable
inscription to be cut upon its face. They have placed
it on the spot where the patriots were buried, and
which, by a happy chance, is in full view from that
whereon is erected the structure which commemorates
the deeds and names of the Cambridge men who fell
in the war of the Rebellion.

We are assembled here this afternoon to dedicate
this Memorial Stone. As we read the inscription that
is borne upon it, we are carried back in imagination
to the days when our Republic was but a bright and
beautiful vision of the future, and not an accomplished
fact ; when our country had no national existence,
but was still a dependency of the British Crown ;
when no flag, brilliant with stars and beaming with
stripes, floated on the breeze to stir the hearts of men

with recollections of past victories; when no strains of martial music encouraged the brave or inspired the timid with valor; when the battles were fought by an undisciplined yeomanry against the trained soldiers of Europe; and when to die for one's country was to be hurried with but little of ceremony, unshrouded and uncoffined, into an unmarked grave. But if these things were true of the " time that tried men's souls," let us, who came here nearly a century later, pour out a measure of gratitude all the more full and fervent. Let us, to whom the Republic is a splendid reality; who are citizens of one of the most powerful nations on the face of the globe; whose eyes are gladdened by the sight of that starry banner, which is the symbol of a country which has proved itself impregnable against the assaults of foreign war and of domestic treason, — let us remember with pride and thankfulness the services of those who laid the foundation stones of this grand temple of American Liberty.

The 19th of April was a sad day for Cambridge. She had lost six of her sons in a single battle, and this when her population was only sixteen hundred souls. Now she numbers forty thousand, and a loss of one hundred and fifty in a battle would be in the same proportion as was a loss of six in the year 1775. It was a sad day; but death must, sooner or later, come to all. It has come to all who saw that struggle. The soldiers, the yeomanry, the agonized women, even the children, — all are gone. But there are six names that survive, and will survive for many a century yet to come. The names of the men who

fell, and who received so unworthy a burial, have
been preserved, and are now recorded imperishably.
To-day we remember them, and are thankful that they
lived and fought.   Soon we, too, shall pass away; but
our successors will take our places, and will bring
here the tribute of grateful hearts.   The stately
Monument which adorns the Common, and the hum-
bler shaft which we have placed here, both speak to
us of patriotism, of devotion to duty, and of self-sacri-
fice in the cause of human rights.   May they carry
down to the latest posterity the story of heroic valor
in the cause of liberty, of justice, and of nationality
created and preserved.

When the Mayor had finished, the choir sung the following original hymn, contributed by Mrs. A. C. WEL-
LINGTON :

> Borne on the ear in accents low
>   From recollection's tide,
> Thought wafts us scenes of early days
>   Which courage beautified.
>
> In solemn consecration met,
>   We tune our melody ;
> Grateful petitions we would raise,
>   And lift our hearts on high.
>
> In mem'ry of that beauteous crown,
>   A patriot's just reward,
> Prized be the fair inheritance
>   Bequeathed to us to guard !
>
> Our fathers fought the glorious fight
>   At Liberty's dear shrine ;
> Affection's tendrils lovingly
>   About this spot shall twine.

The Rev. ALEXANDER McKENZIE then delivered the address which is appended in full. When he had concluded, the ceremonies were closed by singing the following lines, composed for the occasion by Miss SARAH S. JACOBS:

> Now pride and song, and joy and praise,
> Above these graves of other days! —
> Oh, First of our Immortal Dead!
> Whose sons but follow where you led,
>   We come to honor, not to weep;
>   Break not, to-day, your solemn sleep.
>
> Not with war's pomp and mailed breast
> They fought, beneath this sod who rest;
> Like David, with his sling and stone,
> Their trust was in the Lord alone.
>   Their nameless grave has waited long:
>   Its record now make firm and strong.
>
> Swift glide the years with restless haste:
> The crumbling granites bend and waste;
> Yet memory shall, nor changed nor cold,
> This spot in grateful reverence hold;
>   And proudly show, on either hand,
>   Who died to save our native land.

ADDRESS,

BY THE REV. ALEXANDER McKENZIE.

Mr. Mayor and Gentlemen of the City Government;
Fellow-Citizens:

THE doings of this day, interesting and honorable in themselves, have associations which elevate them to a place of high dignity and renown. We have reared this memorial structure to preserve the names and deeds of a few of those who fell in defence of the liberty of the people at the beginning of the long contest which made us a nation. The heroism and devotion of our illustrious sires, which proved the groundwork of our Republic, have long been celebrated in song and story, and recorded among the achievements in which the world glories. Humble was the part which these six men bore in those eventful times; but they stood in their lot, and with a spirit which was equal to more conspicuous performance helped to usher in the grand series of events which changed the destiny of the land, and affected interests as wide as humanity. Their fall counted for more than the deaths of many men in a less important time. We have done well to recog-

3

nize in our national history that which was done on the day we have marked upon this stone, and to give it a foremost place. Concord, Lexington, Menotomy, have long ago erected monuments in memory of those who made their names renowned and that day immortal. At this centre of our early Revolutionary life should rise our column with a kindred purpose, that these men who have deserved well may no longer lie in unmarked graves, but be permitted to tell from the sculptured stone to every passer-by, to those whose homes surround this spot, to the stranger from beyond the seas, on what day and for what cause they rendered up their lives.

The place is well chosen. This stone stands very near the spot where were buried the three who belonged in this part of the town. Trusting to the memory of some who had received the tradition of their burial from the lips of a previous generation, and after careful examination of the ground with results which confirmed the tradition, we may consider it established, with a close approximation to certainty, that we have found and marked the place where these men were laid. When we remember the impossibility of determining where others were buried whose names and virtues we hold in reverence, it is cause for congratulation that we have been able so clearly to mark this resting-place. A few years more, and it could not have been done. Our tardy homage is prudently paid at this time. But it is not for this reason alone that the place is well-chosen. Here are lying the mortal remains of many of our venerated dead. Somewhere in this field of graves is all that is left of the bodily part of Thomas Shepard, who did as much as any man of his time to make Cambridge what it is to-day. Here have been laid many of the Presidents of Harvard College, and many others who were distinguished in different avocations. In the turbulent times of the Revolution some found rest here where no sound of war could reach them. We linger at the humble stones which mark the places where two young men were laid with pains and tears. John Hughes and John Stearns have almost the same epitaph: "He died in his country's cause;" "He died in the service of his country; 1775."

The monument we dedicate to-day stands before the imposing pile we so lately consecrated to its work, which rises from the plain whose very soil is rich in historic associations, and perpetuates the memory of the valor and patriotism of the soldiers and sailors of Cambridge who died in the service of their country in the war for the maintenance of the Union. Truly the stone which now comes to increase the attractions of this ancient burying-ground stands in a glorious place.

The day which has been chosen for this service of patriotism and gratitude fills a marked line in our national annals. On the 3d of November, 1783, the American Army, which had accomplished its purpose and established the land in liberty, was disbanded. On the 20th of the preceding January a general treaty had been signed at Paris. It reminds us of the change in the modes of communication with Europe to read that it was more than two months before the news of peace reached this country. On the 2d of November Washington made his parting address to the armies of the United States. " Never," says one who was present at the breaking up of the army, " never can that melancholy day be forgotten when friends, companions for seven long years in joy and in sorrow, were torn asunder without the hope of ever meeting again, and with prospects of a miserable subsistence in future." On the anniversary of the day which thus closed the war of the Revolution we dedicate a Monument to the memory of men who fell on the day which began it. We bring together events which our national life and history have already united. The story of those early days has been often told. We shall not grow weary of it till we have forgotten its meaning and ceased to be thankful to those who dared and achieved so much. The New-England colonists were Englishmen, with English hearts and hands. They loved liberty, and cherished the recollection of men who were willing to be exiled for its sake, and in their turn were ready to defend it with their lives. They were loyal men, but they never would be slaves. Free principles had grown with their growth. When their prosperity provoked the jealousy of the motherland, and created fears that the Colonies might at length claim independence, efforts were made in England to overturn their political arrangements, and to check their rising manufactures and trade. In justice to the mother-land it 'should be remembered that it was only a portion of the ministerial party in England who projected the measures which oppressed the Colonies and led to their revolution. There were men in high places in England who deserve our admiration and gratitude for their bold assertion of our colonial rights. But baser counsels prevailed.* In 1774 the Boston Port Bill went into operation, with fasting and prayer on the part of the people, with the tolling of bells and prevailing signs of mourning. Other acts were passed in Parliament which deprived the colonists of privileges which they had enjoyed. The interests of the people were protected by the Committees of Correspondence which they had chosen, under whose direction a meeting of delegates was held in Faneuil Hall in August, 1774. "The result was a Provincial Congress, hostile preparation, a clash of arms, and a general rising of the people. To the people of Middlesex County belongs the honor of taking the lead in carrying out the bold plan resolved upon." Four days after the meeting in Faneuil Hall another was held at Concord. The resolves of that meeting ended in this declaration, " No danger shall affright, no difficulties shall intimidate us ; and if, in support of our rights, we are called to encounter even death, we are yet undaunted, sensible that he can never die too soon who lays down his life in support

---

* For historical information I wish to acknowledge my indebtedness to Frothingham's "History of the Siege of Boston," and to the Address of Rev. Samuel Abbot Smith, entitled "West Cambridge on the Nineteenth of April, 1775."

of the laws and liberties of his country." The spirit which prevailed here in those times is still to be seen in our Town Records. At the time of the Stamp Act the Town voted that their Representatives should do nothing to aid in its operation, but use their utmost endeavors to secure its repeal; and "that this vote be recorded in the Town Books, that the children yet unborn may see the desire that their ancestors had for their freedom and happiness."

In 1766 the Representative of the Town in the General Court was instructed to join in respectful addresses to "our most Gracious Sovereign," testifying to the loyalty of the people. He was also to be watchful of any future danger to the Colonies which might arise from the action of Parliament. In 1772 it was voted, "That a Committee be appointed to write to the Committee of the Town of Boston, to acknowledge the vigilance and care discovered by the Metropolis for the public rights and liberties, acquainting them that this Town will heartily concur in all salutary and constitutional measures for the redress of those intolerable grievances which threaten and, if continued, must overthrow the happy civil Constitution of this Province." Two years afterwards it was voted, "That the Committee of Correspondence be a Committee to receive the donations that may be given by the Inhabitants of this Town for the relief of our distressed brethren in the Town of Boston, now suffering for the cause of all America." Two years later still, 1776, May 27, the Representative of the Town was instructed that, if the Honorable Con-

gress should for the safety of the Colonies declare
them independent of the Kingdom of Great Britain,
" We, the said Inhabitants, will solemnly engage
with our lives and fortunes to support them in the
measure." This was the Declaration of Independence
made, in advance of the general action, by the people
of Cambridge.

The example of Middlesex was followed by other
counties. As the determined utterance of Faneuil
Hall was thus repeated on every side, it was plain
that the time for collision had come. General Gage
began at once to fortify Boston Neck. That town of
patriot merchants and mechanics, lawyers and divines,
found itself watched by a hostile fleet, and burdened
with an army whose presence meant intimidation and
oppression. But Boston was brave and decided. The
storm of indignation against the Stamp Act, the fierce
opposition to fresh attempts to impose taxes, the affray
with English soldiers in 1770, the casting overboard of
the taxed tea in 1773, show something of the temper
of the people. In 1774 the first American Conti-
nental Congress assembled, a declaration of rights
was adopted, and a suspension of all commercial
intercourse with Great Britain recommended. About
the same time a Provincial Congress was organized in
Massachusetts which made arrangements for a levy
of twelve thousand men in this State, one-fourth of
whom were to be minute-men. It was more and
more evident that the appeal to arms was to be made.
Minute-men, trained for instant service whenever they
were called, began to spring up through the State;

and there were other preparations for the impending conflict. Gladly would the patriots have averted the war if they could otherwise have maintained their fixed resolve, " America must and will be free."   .

By the middle of April, 1775, Gage had about four thousand men in Boston, when he resolved to make a secret expedition and destroy the colonial magazines at Concord, as the provincial stores at Medford had already been plundered. The preparations which were made attracted the notice of the watchful patriots. Secret plots came to light. On the 18th, the Committees of Safety and of Supplies, which had been organized for the public service, were on the alert, making ready for the anticipated events. They met at Wetherby's tavern in Menotomy. A party of British officers, sent out to guard the roads leading into the country, dined the same day at Cambridge. At night, two lanterns, hung from the steeple of the North Church in Boston, telegraphed across the river the tidings of the movement of the British troops and the direction they were taking. The sexton who lighted the lanterns was afterwards arrested by the British at a funeral, and upon examination condemned to death. A threat of retaliation made by Washington procured his respite, and he was finally exchanged. Richard Devens, of Charlestown, sent to Menotomy and Lexington the news of the advance of the British. Dr. Warren sent Paul Revere, the Boston mechanic, and William Dawes, to alarm the country. Revere crossed the river to Charlestown, while Dawes went out through Roxbury. They met

at Lexington, where Hancock and Adams were in
waiting. The messengers hurried on to arouse the
people beyond. As the news spread, the people
prepared for the emergency which was upon them.
Many secured their most valuable possessions, in some
cases making their wells their treasury. The women
and children, the old and infirm, were removed to
secure places. The men awaited their foes.

Meanwhile, the British troops, numbering about
eight hundred, and commanded by Lieutenant-Colonel
Smith, about ten o'clock in the evening embarked at
the foot of Boston Common, and landed at Phipps's
farm, now Lechmere Point. They struck across the
marshes to the old road from Charlestown to West
Cambridge, and proceeded on their way. They soon
found that the country was alarmed. Many persons
saw them and heard them. It was almost two o'clock
in the clear, chilly morning of the 19th of April, when
they reached West Cambridge. Vice-President Gerry,
and Colonels Lee and Orne who were with him, all
of whom were members of the Committee of Safety,
very nearly fell into their hands. At the centre of
the town the troops halted. As it was evident that
their task was larger than they had anticipated, a
messenger was sent back to Boston to ask for reinforcements. A detachment of six companies of
light infantry, under command of Major Pitcairn, was
ordered forward to Concord. These pressed on,
arresting every man they met. One of their prisoners
escaping carried to Lexington the first certain news
of their approach. Pitcairn found some sixty or

seventy of the militia drawn up near the Lexington meeting-house, and with them about forty spectators, a few of whom were armed. The British troops rushed on, shouting and firing; and the officers cried out: "Ye villains! ye rebels! disperse! Lay down your arms! Why don't you lay down your arms?" Finding the demand unheeded, they fired, doing no harm. They fired again, and men fell. Then the militia, who had been ordered not to fire unless they were fired upon, returned the assault of the troops. Resistance was so clearly in vain, that the militia withdrew, fired upon as long as they remained in sight. Seven were killed and ten wounded on the American side. The British, with huzzas over their easy victory, hastened on to Concord. They might shout, but they had begun a work whose end would be their own undoing. There was cause for rejoicing, but it was not with them. The prophetic vision of Samuel Adams looked through the dark days which were at hand to the exceeding light and liberty beyond, and he uttered the lofty exclamation which we have written in granite: "Oh, what a glorious morning is this!"

It was a short march to Concord; but there the work of destruction which had brought the British from Boston met with small success. They broke open about sixty barrels of flour, disabled a few cannon, cut down the liberty-pole, set the court-house on fire; but the greater part of the military stores, which had been collected at Concord had been previously concealed, or removed to other places out of the reach of the

enemy. The tidings of the approach of the British
had brought to Concord the minute-men from the
neighboring towns. The surrounding communities
were inflamed with enthusiasm, convinced that the
hour had come when they must defend their rights
with their lives. The training which the people had
received, in their contests with the Indians and the
French, fitted them for the sterner work now laid
upon them. Muskets which had seen service at Louis-
burg and Quebec came forth to new duty; drums
which had followed the British flag to honorable
battle beat along the country roads which led to the
scene of peril. The fathers lived again in their sons.
The patriots and a portion of the invaders met at the
river by the North Bridge. The British fired upon
the people. The guns of the minute-men answered
them. Men fell on both sides. The conflict was
brief, when the detachment of the British retreated
upon their main forces, pursued by the provincials.
Meanwhile the number of the colonial force was
increasing. The British acted upon their discretion,
and, having hastily buried their dead in the public
square, about noon began their march back to Boston.
It was a perilous march. From out the woods at the
side of the road, from behind trees and walls, the
murderous fire poured upon the retreating troops.
Panic took the place of order. Many began to run.
The officers went in front and threatened with death
every man who advanced. But nothing could have
averted surrender or utter destruction but the timely
arrival of the reinforcements which had been re-

quested. These formed a hollow square, and received
the weary, affrighted men. "They were so much
exhausted with fatigue," says a British historian, "that
they were obliged to lie down for rest on the ground,
their tongues hanging out of their mouths like those
of dogs after a chase." Dr. Warren and General
Heath were busy directing the movements of the
militia and encouraging them in their grand under-
taking. Later in the day, in West Cambridge, Warren
had a pin struck out of the hair of his earlock. So near
did death come to him before Bunker Hill had given
him his riper fame. Lord Percy had come, with some
eighteen hundred veteran troops and two field-pieces,
to succor the earlier detachment, now fugitives. He
came through Roxbury, showing his confidence
by the tune of Yankee Doodle, to which his troops
marched, and disturbing the country through which
he passed. The selectmen of Cambridge had taken
up the planks of the Great Bridge in what is now
Brighton Street. In order to prevent the retreat of
the British in that direction, Warren had directed the
militia to use the planks as a barricade. But as they
had been left on this side of the river, it was an easy
matter for the British to replace them, when the troops
passed over, hurried along our North Avenue, and
met their defeated brethren near the Lexington meeting-house.

In connection with this expedition is an incident
more to the credit of our town. A convoy of provisions found greater difficulty in crossing the bridge,
and became detached from the main army. An ex-

press was sent from Old Cambridge to Menotomy, announcing the coming of these supplies, and a few men, too old for active service in the field, posted themselves behind a wall to await their arrival. The convoy came, and was called upon to surrender. The drivers whipped up their horses. The provincials fired, killing several horses, and perhaps two men, when the drivers jumped from their places and fled. The wagons were secured and plundered. The drivers are said to have surrendered themselves to an old woman whom they met, whose protection they begged. Whereupon there went the rounds of the English papers belonging to the opposition that interesting sum in the Rule of Three: "If one old Yankee woman can take six grenadiers, how many soldiers will it require to conquer America?" "So to West Cambridge belongs the honor of making the first capture of provisions and stores, and also of prisoners, in the American Revolution."

The march of the British troops back to Boston was resumed. They committed much destruction, pillaging and burning buildings, and grossly abusing individuals who fell in their power. They were stung by defeat, full of anger and revenge, glad to let their passions loose, though the helpless were the chief sufferers. It was a memorable retreat, and many sad incidents of it are preserved in the family traditions of those who lived along its route. The skirmishing in West Cambridge was fierce and bloody. The people were excited by the outrages committed by the troops, who on their part were contending with enemies often invisible, and were struggling for life in the midst of disgrace. The British took the road around Prospect Hill. They were embarrassed by the wounded they were obliged to carry. The provincials followed them closely, and were increasing in numbers. The British came down the Cambridge road to Charlestown Neck almost upon the run, so anxious were they to get within the protection of their ships of war. When Charlestown Common was reached, the pursuit was stopped. The reports of the day show, as the American losses, forty-nine killed, thirty-nine wounded, five missing. On the part of the British there were seventy-three killed, one hundred and seventy-four wounded, twenty-six missing, most of whom were prisoners. The enlistment-rolls of the minute company of West Cambridge, comprising probably the names of all the men in that precinct of suitable age, are still preserved. They contain fifty names, — one-half of which are marked Cambridge. Benjamin Locke was captain of the company which did good service at Lexington.

It is impossible to take out of the doings of the day the share in the good work which belongs to this part of Cambridge. We may be content to feel that those who were before us were united to their neighbors in spirit and in deed. The desolation of the town, the deserted wives and children, tell us where the men were. It is pleasant for us to remember that our domain was wider then than now, and with a worthy pride we claim the glory of Menotomy for the praise of Cambridge. There is something in these ancient associations, in the brave deeds which have been wrought out under the good old name, within the old municipality, which creates and encourages the hope that our friends who have gone out from us will yet be numbered with us again, that our heir-looms of historic places and achievements may be a common possession.   It was in recognition of our former estate, and with pride in it, that, when called upon to furnish the inscription for the monument we have now erected, I recommended that the names of three men who are buried in the old Second Precinct should be inscribed upon it.   Arlington may guard their dust.   Cambridge will overleap the narrow brook, and claim them for her own.

That was a terrible night here which preceded the day of which we speak.   Hannah Winthrop has written something of " the horrors of that midnight cry, preceding the battle of Lexington."   It shows us Cambridge.   " A few hours, with the dawning day, convinced us the bloody purpose was executing; the platoon-firing assuring us the rising sun must witness the bloody carnage.   Not knowing what the event would be at Cambridge at the return of these bloody ruffians, and seeing another brigade despatched to the assistance of the former, looking with the ferocity of barbarians, it seemed necessary to retire to some place of safety.   We set out, not knowing whither we went.   We were directed to a place called Fresh Pond; but what a distressed house did we find it! — filled with women whose husbands had gone forth to meet the assailants, seventy or eighty of these (with

numberless infant children) weeping and agonizing
for the fate of their husbands. In addition to these
signs of distress, we were for some time in sight of
the battle; the glittering instruments of death pro-
claiming by an incessant fire that much blood must
be shed, that many widowed and orphaned ones must
be left as monuments of British barbarity." It was
unsafe to return to their homes, and they were hastily
sent to Andover. "Thus we began our pilgrimage,
alternately walking and riding, the road filled with
frighted women and children. But what added greatly
to the horrors of the scene was our passing through
the bloody field at Menotomy, which was strewed with
the mangled bodies." Thus writes one to whom the
deeds and sufferings we recount were a present, personal reality. That assemblage of affrighted women
bears plain testimony to the part the men of Cambridge were taking. Her vivid portraiture brings
before us one side of the scenes in which these men,
whose names we have cut in stone, bore a part, and
reminds us of the agony and anxiety of those to whom
they were bound by the closest ties, — who watched
their going out and waited for their coming back,
who lost sight of the forms which were so dear to
them beneath this freshly hallowed sod. There is a
glimpse of the anxiety and commotion of the night
which closed upon that glorious though fated day, in
the haste with which our three men were buried.
The son of John Hicks, a boy fourteen years old, was
sent by his mother in the afternoon to look for his
father who had been absent most of the day. He

found him lying by the side of the road dead. Marcy and Richardson were near him. He procured assistance, and the bodies were lifted into a wagon and brought here for burial. But who had leisure for funeral rites? The dead alone were safe, done with duty. The living had the living to care for. One grave received them all, as with patriotic indignation against the tyranny and cruelty which hurried them to their death, with admiration and affection for their devotion to the common weal, they were given to the keeping of their mother-earth. The son of Moses Richardson, standing by, thought it was too bad that the earth should be thrown directly upon their faces, and getting into the trench he spread the large cape of his father's coat over his face.

"Not a drum was heard, not a funeral note,
 As his corse to the rampart we hurried;
Not a soldier discharged his farewell shot
 O'er the grave where our hero we buried.

"No useless coffin enclosed his breast,
 Not in sheet nor in shroud we wound him;
But he lay, like a warrior, taking his rest,
 With his martial cloak around him!

"Slowly and sadly we laid him down,
 From the field of his fame fresh and gory;
We carved not a line, and we raised not a stone,
 But we left him alone with his glory."

The day has come when a grateful posterity blesses their memory and honors their rest.

It seems strange to us that veteran British troops should have been defeated by the irregular forces opposed to them. We must acknowledge the purpose and working of Him who first brought our Fathers to these shores and made them a people. We must recognize the power there is in a good cause.

" What stronger breastplate than a heart untainted!
Thrice is he arm'd that hath his quarrel just."

The conviction that they were fighting for liberty, for the honor of their land, the safety of their homes, the inheritance of their children, gave them a spirit which in itself was discipline, and a daring which was a good substitute for men. It has been finely said, " The people always conquer. They always must conquer. . . . God never gave, and never will give, a final triumph over a virtuous and gallant people, resolved to be free." It must be kept in mind, also, that they were in some measure prepared for their work. We have seen that it was by slow degrees that war approached and became inevitable. Men banded themselves together in anticipation of the time of need. Militia and minute-men were placed in the best posture of defence. The warlike training of other times was made to serve in the new exigencies. It is true that Washington was disappointed at the condition of the American Army when he assumed command. There were not many more than fourteen thousand men under arms against the well-appointed British troops. Even to his eye they seemed but raw militia. Yet there was more of training than appeared, more of system and agreement. The fighting on the 19th of April was irregular; but it was with one purpose, and with the help of organization. There were leaders and followers. Lord Percy said " he never saw any thing equal to the intrepidity of the minute-men." There was skill in the leaders which carried the courage to a successful issue. The British fought that day, especially on their retreat, not alone against actual men, but against imaginary enemies. Men seemed to drop from the clouds. Any peaceful stone-wall might be a fortress, and the quiet grove mask a battery. One old gray-headed man of Woburn figures in the stories of the time, who rode a fine white horse after the flying troops, and dismounting within gunshot would send his sure bullet to the mark. When he fired, a man fell. They came to cry at sight of him, " Look out, there is the man on the white horse!" Even the multitudes of the old and infirm, of women and children, looking down from the hillsides, were transformed to their frightened imagination into hosts of armed men threatening their extinction. Amid the unknown terrors which beset these strangers in a strange land, with lurking foes on every side, with all the country pouring its forces against them, it is hardly strange that they lost hope and daring, and fled in panic and alarm.

This day would have been memorable in itself; but it has justly attained a wider and higher renown because it opened the War of the Revolution. Purposes had passed into deeds. Both patriots and invaders had gone too far to recede and leave things as they had been. Blood had been shed. A spirit had been evoked which could not be put down. The end praises the beginning. We have become so accustomed to immense armies, that the men engaged on that glorious April day seem to us very few. Yet they bore no mean proportion to the whole force of the war of our Independence, and their endeavor and their deeds were large. The prowess which was displayed was the earnest of the persistence and valor which many weary years could not exhaust. The success which crowned the opening struggle held the presage of grander results which were to follow and give us a name among the nations of the earth. We share in the glory of the after-time which our Fathers helped bring to the land; and the places among which we move day by day were the scenes of many of the great events of our heroic age. Yet proud as we are, in common with all the country, of the accomplishments of the later times, we shall cherish with fond, personal interest the thrilling memories of the battle of Concord, Lexington, and Cambridge. There has been power in the names. They have done much to create and foster a national feeling. Not territory, laws, institutions, alone unite us, but the fields where our Fathers fought, the days they illumined with their valor, the names they made immortal. Our national estate is partly in our national history. Blot out our past, and we should be a different and a poorer people, though we kept all our material and intellectual wealth. We need our heroes. We shall never be done with our honored dead. Sad will be the time when we cease to be instructed by their example, inspirited by every thought of them.

No wide expanse of domain, no annexation of new countries, could enrich us so largely as the narrow fields whereon our liberty was bought with blood. Plymouth Rock is better for us than a mountain of gold. Through the war which so lately closed behind us the force of the earlier contest for liberty was felt. Out of the struggles which made us a nation passed an energy to keep us a nation. Do you not recall the words spoken by our martyred President at his first inauguration when men were threatening rebellion and dissolution? "The mystic cord of memory, stretching from every battle-field and patriot grave to every living heart and hearth-stone all over this broad land, will yet swell the chorus of the Union." It rolled on through the smoke of battle, amid the roar of artillery; but blending in that chorus as it was sung over the land, over the sea, were the names of Concord and Bunker Hill, were the deeds of which every child learns to boast, and which every man recounts with honest pride.

It is fitting that this stone should confront our more imposing monument. Smaller is this, few the names upon it, modest its pretension; yet it may stand boldly before the people, and overlook the ancient training-field, and face the pile which towers above it. For out of that which these men and their associates accomplished rose the nation which those men defended and preserved. It was one cause. Ninety years are little in the world's history. We may write on both monuments, These men died for our country.

Of all the treasured names of that land from which has come the beautiful stone we have now reared and dedicated, none is dearer to us than his who has written thus of Old Mortality: "He considered himself as fulfilling a sacred duty, while renewing to the eyes of posterity the decaying emblems of the zeal and sufferings of their forefathers, and thereby trimming, as it were, the beacon-light, which was to warn future generations to defend their religion even unto blood."

Take Scotland's message with Scotland's stone! As we revive the zeal and sufferings of our forefathers, and write them plainly before the world, trimming our beacon-light, let it be that we may defend the liberties they have bequeathed, in the spirit with which they won them for us, and transmit them a legacy unimpaired, improved with our doings, for the blessing of all who shall come after us.

NOTE.

In the effort to find the precise place in which the three men of Cambridge were buried, there was found a piece of cloth, deeply marked with reddish-brown stains, which was thought to be a piece of the clothing of one of the men, and to be stained with his blood. A portion of this cloth was submitted to Professor Horsford for his critical examination; and the results at which he arrived are stated in the following letter:

CAMBRIDGE, Dec. 22, 1870.

REV. ALEXANDER MCKENZIE:

My DEAR SIR, — The interesting relic, in regard to which you have asked my judgment, has been subjected to such examination and chemical tests as naturally suggested themselves.

It is, in the first place, a frail little piece of dull reddish-brown cloth, about four inches by five, such as might have been spun and woven in the year 1775. One margin presents the even edge of warp, as if it had been cut with shears as linen is cut, and not torn as cotton cloth usually is. It presents occasional broken folds and small holes where fragments have dropped out, — the record of decay. More than two-thirds of the surface is marked by dark reddish stains.

As tradition tells the story, this fragment of cloth may have been part of the shirt or handkerchief that absorbed the blood of one of the minute-men of Cambridge who fell on the day of the battle of Lexington, and in the exigency of the times had been buried in the suit he wore. He had gone out after Lord Percy had marched up the North Avenue, and had been shot by a flanking party of the returning British army. This tradition is fully confirmed by my examination.

The microscope shows the fibre of the cloth to be *linen*. The portions of the cloth which are free from stain, when burned, give the odor common to the smoke of simple *vegetable fibre*, as cotton or linen. But the portions which are *stained*, when burned, give the odor of burning *animal* matter, as of feathers or hair or horn. Now, if these stains are stains of blood, which contains *fibrine*, which is of the same nature as hair or horn, such odor might be expected to arise from burning. In a dry, sandy soil, dried fibrine would resist decay quite as long as the linen fibre or as the woollen fibre of the outer garment which was found with this fragment. The blood and its fibrine had had ample time to dry before the body was found. How long such dried animal matter would resist decay is illustrated in the mummies of Mexico and Peru. The structure of the minute corpuscles of the blood would be likely to perish, and the microscope does not reveal them; but the chemical constituents imbedded in, and a part of, the fibrine would remain; and for certain of them we have, in chemistry, very delicate tests. Two of them, *iron* and *phosphoric acid*, I looked for, and found without difficulty. Soda, which is a constituent of the blood, is, however, also present in all soils, and in the dust of every apartment; and so its recognition in the cloth would have little weight. Perhaps the same objection applies in some degree to the iron. But a porous, sandy soil would yield no evidence of phosphoric acid to such tests as I employed.

Taking these results into account, in connection with the circumstance that the little piece of blotched linen cloth was found with other cloth of woollen, — was found with human bones, in a dry, sandy soil, at but a short depth from the surface, in the very place where a gentleman, who died a few years ago at great age, said he had assisted in burying the body of his father in the clothes which he wore when he fell on the fatal day, — taking all these considerations into account, there can, I think, be no doubt that I have before me veritable blood of the first that was shed in the great war of the Revolution.

I am very truly yours,

E. N. HORSFORD.

We may be confident, it appears, that we have an interesting relic of the memorable day to which this publication refers, and are permitted to look upon blood which was shed in defence of our liberties.

ALEXANDER McKENZIE.

CAMBRIDGE, 22d December, 1870.

Cambridge: Press of John Wilson & Son.